I am, am I,
to trust
the joy
that joy is
no more
or less
there now
than before

I am, am I,
to trust
the joy
that joy is
no more
or less
there now
than before

Evan Kennedy

ROOF BOOKS
NEW YORK

ISBN: 978-1-931824-87-3
Library of Congress Control Number: 2020945817

Cover photograph by Ryan Darley

Acknowledgments: Several texts previously appeared in *baest*, *The Beauty Salons: Writers at Aeromoto*, and *Dispatches from the Poetry Wars*. Deep thanks to their editors.

for my friends

 This project is supported, in part, by an award from the National Endowment for the Arts.

 This book is made possible, in part, by the New York State Council on the Arts with the support of Governor Andrew Cuomo and the New York State Legislature.

Roof Books
are published by
Segue Foundation
300 Bowery, New York, NY 10012
seguefoundation.com

Roof Books
are distributed by
Small Press Distribution
1341 Seventh Street
Berkeley, CA. 94710-1403
800-869-7553 or spdbooks.org

Table of Contents

Runt Savant

I live in the time that follows the invention of the bicycle, so when it is dusk, I can be seen pedaling from the crowd.

The street is level though the planet may not be.

Subject to innumerable laws, I expect violence from some I see; from others, I expect no more than permission to continue cycling, which is all I request.

Of course I am tempted to run red lights as though racing my regrets.

An accounting takes place in my average-sized brain while the street numbers increase.

Though I would like to do so, it is dangerous while pedaling to study anything in the tactile world: I would be bound to wreck.

One exception is the straining, bare calves of the cyclists in front.

I synchronize my exertions to the shadows leaping with their pedaling.

Police idle like the fog and obscure my vision.

For some, this is a leisure city, however much I sweat on the incline that slowly develops.

A breath of queenly grace straightens the backs of those able to be leisurely, while others wait to be made able.

I am not quite here, as everyone can see.

I am still in disbelief that the alphabet before you stands in for the sounds that I have been making.

While cycling, I am in a kicking fetal position arriving at the following moment.

I may as well have never left the womb.

My black jacket and the small silver body, a pendant against my chest, are my I.D.; my sweet and scowling face is my I.D.

I wish to be admitted continually to a gentler order.

My panting is a kind of script: a writing that secures me among my readers who hold me bodily in sight.

My eyes display a kind of writing read by attentive passersby.

It is idiotic to think that my genitals are enough of an alphabet in situations when I am taken by desire, yet it might be enough when I best enact my affinities.

I still have a reason to believe I will be delivered.

I arrived at this belief through everyday positions, locked lips, and a kind of transience.

I absolutely feel love for creation.

It stands in for song.

As far as I understand these sights, they are mine, and as far as I do not, they are, I suppose, God's.

I am at a red light, and my heat is my transpiring.

❋

When I as an infant soiled myself, my mother or father would do the changing. I was gently brought into several positions that had become quite familiar. I was set on my back, lifted by my feet, rolled to my side then to the other. I cannot remember more. Perhaps my account would be more faithfully articulated if I ever changed another. The dog barked. I had not yet felt shame. At the moment of changing, my comfort was assured, so I wonder how a mother or father could fear for their child, because enough has been given, hasn't it, though I admit that I am still childless to this very moment. Such are the limits to the fruits of my experience. Innocence is expired, though an existence has been framed by the caring actions from this time.

✹

My brain had not yet developed ways to distinguish the world. Any sound I made was an early attempt at differentiation. Whatever blather I ascribed to an object was its name, though I may have called it something else the following day. My mind had not developed enough to understand that I was wrong (it still may not have developed to understand this), so I could not know that my mother, for instance, had abilities to communicate that far exceeded mine. She was understood. The notion that I was trapped in a nonoperational body incapable of being understood should have been terrifying, though I believe that nothing of the sort came to my mind.

Today, there may be the statement that my body had been, or still is, nonoperational, or not as operational and sensate as I should like, then something comes along to keep me from staring at my roots. I become distracted by something I cannot identify.

✹

Though received by love, I was born ruined; though received by ruin, I was born loved.

11

The reach of my recollection and anticipation was not very far. Each was as short as the arms extending from me, and as unreliable. Though frail, I often smiled when asleep or awake. I may have been rooting out my faults, but my demands became numerous. I learned speech to keep up. Then I learned to read. Childhood overtook my infancy, replaced some of my cells, and developed others so that I grew.

It could be said that childhood swiped my infancy and made me its very own. I took on the perspectives of different people, animals, and things, even classmates, and developed empathy to counter my potential for violence. I was asking my dog who made it.

※

Lessons in counting included drawings of numbers and their spelling alongside animals in a signifying quantity. Or there was a song, a melody I still recall. I may have clapped my hands in the way I applaud instances of your brilliance today.

It is unclear why the alphabet is in its order, or who ordered it, yet the sequence of numbers was obvious and offered a logic that language cannot yet bring me.

※

The teacher walked around trying in one quick movement to swipe whatever we were using to write. If it could not be taken, there was the assumption that we held it too strongly, inviting fatigue in our hands. My fingernails would and still to this day whiten with the pressure I exert while writing. Before it can depart, I force my thought onto the page. I was one of the few issued a corrective grip.

※

I could not have been born knowing that I was created. The idea must have arrived just after my infancy. A part of myself must have guided me to this realization. This part understands that I, a totality of parts, was created, though I cannot explain its reasoning or why it is so certain.

There are enough obstructions between myself and this idea that I may only reach it and say, *There you are*, or some other greeting, before thinking something else, or I spend many days invoking the notion and the direction it indicates yet never feel it resonate.

✳

When I was learning to read, an adult asked me how I determined the meaning of an unfamiliar word within a sentence. I tried to say that its meaning can be found within the words surrounding it. I meant that a word is surrounded by reasons it was selected, though I had been skipping the unfamiliar word without giving it much consideration. The word in question did not yet pertain to me, because I had yet to speak or hear it. I was wishing to preserve my joy as it had been articulated by me, and if, when I was speaking, the new word happened to find its way into my mouth, in whatever definition I intended, I understood that I had left the door to my world *unfastened*.

✳

I take a new book and inscribe it with my day and the demands in my upkeep. Hydration is one demand of this body, so it should surprise no one when droplets fall into my book. Even one move can warp its pages.

My memory is not very dependable, so I make faint pencil marks alongside helpful or inspiring passages. I figure it is better that a book be marked up by me than shelved by someone about to collapse from boredom.

13

A common emission among the living is the oily imprinting by palms, forehead, even chest and thighs. My palms often smudge ink from the pages onto the book's sides. A reader like me is little more than a smudger, working tenderly in the world and its approximations.

I have no idea who works behind me to clean up my everyday mess, but my book is a mop that accelerates its efforts at absorbing my fluids whenever I accelerate my destructing body. My book is a bib, rag, or chestplate. Thanks to its defenses, I could finish the day in fine shape, like I just toweled off from the bath that begins my morning.

Whatever could compromise people's first impression of me is minimized by my book's terrific ability to take such a beating. I would never be able to sell it to anyone. A bookseller would take one look at its condition and know that I had been through a battle informed by its contents. I should not even try to part with it but instead return it to my disorderly shelf.

✳

I realize the possibility that the sentence I have just spoken has never been said on Earth. I think to myself: *What could have happened in the world for this sentence to be spoken?* I do not even talk much, yet there I was in a rare moment of stringing sentences together, with all the required elements, and I spoke a sentence that had never been heard by anyone. And I felt altered along with the world, though it would be dishonest if I were to say that it was by very much at all.

✳

I look to a listener for an indication that I have been heard, even understood. Voice emerges from an intimate part of the body, and I may speak feeling ashamed, brazen, embarrassed, impaired, indifferent, maladapted, or uncertain. Often with incomplete sentences. Or I end a sentence with *so...*

The distance between sensation and its articulation is the cause of so much of my worry, and yes, reconciliation, especially when the dynamic of the social is at play among listeners with whom I spend this tremendous time, and those I regret ever having met.

*

To this day, I neglect to look up unfamiliar words, or I forget the ones I know, and feel enough embarrassment when I am corrected that I stop speaking, or I silently consider pronunciation, and my interlocutor begins a different topic. I shy before those who speak well, or quickly, or those who are talented in new languages. Theirs is not a society that includes me unless they happen to feel generous for the moment.

Maybe I should refuse the expansion of my vocabulary since the stations of my argument must be plain, conceived in a stutter, and approach the ornament of basic grammar, if there is much ornament to the lyric that will replace my body.

*

I was first brought to a church for a classmate's baptism, an entirely unfamiliar occasion. I have no memory of what my mother may have said to prepare me—it is a pity since our forgetfulness must prolong the suffering of our mothers. The room for the baptism was unremarkable. It suited the god-fearing, who were difficult to understand but easy to joke about—it took many years until I realized that many of them were my enemies.

Before a crucifix, another first, I began breaking my teeth on scraps of a conversation that continues today. I only knew about the birth, so I completed a narrative that worked toward the adult body of sorrow grieving before me. I was sensitive, so it was easy to pity. Nobody bleeding like that could have much command over their lives, but I also mistrusted recipients of violence. They could appear to me somehow complicit.

I remember how out of place, almost feral, I must have looked to my neighbors. The miniature outfit worn by my friend struck me as wasteful because soon it would be outgrown, though it was amazing how a new item of clothing leant the day an undeniable solemnity that paid for itself many times over. I realize that I have no clothes that can lend me my neighbor's fantastic solemnity from that day.

Sometimes I sit on the floor and draw my knees to my chest. My body almost splits in two when I remember how my friend's suit looked ruined by the water that was administered. I was astonished to see the clothing clinging to a baptized body to enact a drowning or removal from the world. I felt a little drowned as well. Something brushed past my ear, and the sensation of eternity sunk a little into our bones. The idea of obedience became very appealing with its hunch that reward can be delayed to either the following minute or our death from old age.

✳

I would like to meet again what was in me from the start of my life and identical to the responses of those I love. One day I might be found a complete embodiment of that serenity, perhaps stilled in accompaniment, attentive as nature. Perhaps something from the air will exert upon me the kindness I could bring to my interactions along the earth's surface in the way that a leaf on a branch on a tree can indicate the graces of a formal garden. Anything I learned has made the earth quiver, not me.

✳

What I miss most about childhood is participating in the creation of a classroom, the unity of characters that the teacher, little more than an outsider, would call *a good class* or *a bad class*.

The first weeks were a time of formlessness. We carefully arranged ourselves into parts of a singular body. Each child became, say, an arm, ear, intestine, organ, or uvula of the class. Our collaboration was silent, however vocal we must have been during learning. At times, it was as though we could read one another's minds, attack or console one another with a glance. Obedience and disobedience were twin deities who put a shine onto our existence.

All this looked helpful to our futures, but what we really needed was someone to take us each by the hand and lead us out of the classroom and into the conduct of individual learners. I only arrived at that conduct by deserting the pact made in my classrooms.

✳

I had thought my eyes were perfect spheres until I discovered the corneas that could be felt by my finger once I closed my eyelids to examine this essential triumph of my anatomy. Perhaps this was the only instance when my eyelids closed to assist an examination. I closed my eyes, placed a finger upon my upper eyelids, and shifted my eyes again and again to the left then right. Though these were the same motions everyone in the world uses to read, or most, or at least very many, I was only reading through my fingertips the surface of the organs that allowed my entrance into a world exceeding my capacities for adulation.

✳

When I was a child volunteer at the hospital, my peers fought over positions in the maternity ward. I spent my assignment in the emergency room wearing an approximation of a white uniform. I chose this position so I could witness the drama of life. To be specific, I expected something to register on my nervous system toward a deeper acquaintance with the workings of human bodies.

Being helpful was also an interest, yet my hours there were unspeakably boring. Emergencies, if what I saw could qualify as emergencies, were few and far between. I stocked shelves and sat at the front desk beside the nurse receptionist.

My face took on the tense mask of impatience, all too frequently worn through my youth. It was implied that I was training for the position I would occupy as an adult, and if the hospital meant to prepare me for a life at a desk delivering my mind to the prospect of sensation's arrival, they left me sufficiently prepared.

When the nurse receptionist asked if I would like to see a fresh cadaver as a way of informing my future career, I declined with a shyness that adults often confused with good manners. I had already learned more than I could have anticipated.

※

An hour of tutoring was offered early on the morning of every algebra test. We sat anywhere we could or stood in the back. It was still dark outside. Within us began a battle to waken our attention while our teacher solved equations on an overhead projector. Because the room was kept dark so we could read the exercises, my classmates tended to fall back asleep. It was gratifying to see that happen because it meant that I had the upper hand if I could rally my concentration.

Our teacher ran through every variety of problem we would encounter on the test, and occasionally allude to the test itself with warnings and insights only its creator could provide. I never fell asleep, but I watched my mind fail, excuse itself, and ache as it reached verifiable truths. I saw plotted within me some points of comprehension that were always threatening to vanish. I would need to shape my behavior to those points.

It was too early in life to refer to myself as bright. I only projected uncertainty into whatever room I entered. Set before me was a process through which I could only begin to measure my potential.

✳

I give innumerable animals a scratch behind the ears, tear apart and devour the carcasses of almost as many.

I wave hello to innocence when I see it strolling on a Sunday.

(If Sunday is the only day when one is able to stroll, I have found the task of lyric: to open the other six days to this prospect.)

Meanwhile, others try to devour me, for better or worse, and I pull myself from their mouths, and maybe I make an ugly gesture.

It is as though I train to hold the reins of a decorated animal taking me into the future, though my future is beginning to look uncertain.

Past disasters and insights are never entirely let go.

I cradle a head that is a composite of all my romances.

The face could use a wash, but its serenity indicates a mother who is loved.

✳

Puberty was a time when I wished to leave vertically from humans. I had the sensation of levitating within my contempt and awe. It could be said that adolescence swiped my childhood and made me its very own. I felt I was losing a body but got the hint that things were starting to fill out. Even a little danger loved was death won. I saw some classmates become docile within this danger as I have friends today who are still docile within it. Sex held little promise.

My heart kept a certain hope that my young demands could be sustained through those years. These demands, it was hoped, would rise in response to whatever would compromise my innocence.

I learned to correctly spell that last word, in particular the number of c's (two) versus the number of s's (none). Its spelling helped complete a maturation that could surround and defend the remnant of my childlike form and thinking.

✳

Even when clean, my clothes act like me, the integrated and circulatory creature before you. My clothes can articulate my positions through their collars, cuffs, and buttons, my hems, buckles, pockets, flies, and clasps, my jacket which I zip up to lend authority to my compliments and complaints.

When my clothing and I are in formation, we appear like newlyweds or twins. We finish each other's sentences. It embraces or restrains me. Its dimensions and my own are commensurate. The residue of what I engage becomes an accessory on me.

✳

Sometimes an hour in the bathtub makes me feel dirtier, or less myself. There is something troubling when my natural scent, favored by many animals and humans, is lost. With worry over losing my essence, I watch the water become discolored. Perhaps dirt, or the exertion to excrete it, is my condition. A few I sleep with prefer me unbathed by a few days, and perhaps I should defer to them. There are times I spend bathing, in a manner of speaking, in other things, and I wonder how I emerge. I go through the day and understand that I bathed in a procession, a destiny, a sacrament, or a wave. I save my items from these excursions to prove that I was immersed. I try to reach an ideal condition, or the understanding that I may never get clean, whatever connotation that word assumes.

✻

While paddling a kayak back to shore, I was not strong enough to keep the bow perpendicular to the tide, and in an instant, I was flipped upside-down. The sound of my head hitting the water stays with me, cataloged in my mind among other incidents when I encountered an unforgiving surface. I was wearing a kind of skirt that secured myself within the boat. Its purpose was to prevent water from entering, but once upside-down, I found that I was not strong enough to release myself.

I had no time to wait for my strength to return, though I might still be waiting it out to this moment, holding my breath for a flash of light, an idea really, to rescue me again. During my boating mishap, my breath was giving out and my brain felt to be approaching some kind of equilibrium with the water. I was all pulse and reeling, and suddenly under this strain, or distention of time, I became stilled for a moment.

The notion arose that around me nothing shared my danger. I felt division and a deep loneliness, a feeling that could return during the hours before I die, presuming that I have no company alongside me declining at a comparable rate. I started to doubt that I was upside-down. Nor did I believe that I was in a situation that birthed me into a peripheral world and its dangers.

As I was moments from giving up the suppression of my breathing, my body slackened, the pressure enclosed me, and imposed upon me somehow was the success of extricating myself. I had been detached still wearing the skirt.

＊

When I am inattentive, I am removed from the day and its options for watchfulness. I see the labor of my eyes then greet that observation before it leaves me. Around me develops a land or narrative. It soon passes, and I am not the arrow toward anything. I realize that I am not exactly inattentive but distracted. What I should not be welcoming has arrived. I tilt my head to the angle people use when indecisive, then I engage my distraction to keep it from leaving. Various parts of my body differ in their desire for distraction as much as they feel to differ in temperature. My hands may want what my feet refuse. My answer to all this stands nearby. My answer may even be waving to me. Though my body offers the chance to get out of this, I have not taken up its offer.

I would learn less about myself if I looked in a mirror. My distraction and I are so similar we both have dreamy eyes. A voice from outside points out the vanity of my distraction, but I have not heard it. I am now tapped on the shoulder by the answer to all this, but I do not turn yet.

＊

A description of my face should not be offered, yet I am now observing my reflection and find the moment opportune for a self-portrait. With the light behind me, the edges of my ears become illuminated, and so I almost hear the realization, like it is spoken aloud, that my face is better framed than I thought. It appears precise. It appears almost lovingly outlined.

My eyes appear to retreat into my skull. I can almost watch this happen. I anticipate the observation that my features stand *livingly reserved*. The rest is *a passive and gentle mass*, while behind my closed lips, my tongue thrashes. To contain this activity, the corners of my lips tighten slightly. Only the most receptive and delicate nerves within the flesh of my face perceive it. My nostrils broaden to extend my life; my facial expressions carry a trace of this future.

I reach the understanding that my expressions may have been influenced by being observed, and with this understanding, the interest in offering a description of my face dissipates on the verge of its fulfillment.

※

My sibling and I started to look alike while the intervals between our visits lengthened. I said nothing, though strangers too must have noticed the resemblance. A few years earlier, my sibling and I could appear in public and lend little impression we were related. We certainly did not resemble our parents. Relatives further back, vague names, had a slight resemblance to my sibling and I, though this implied no kinship, at least for me. I sensed they carried no resemblance to my inner life, my systems of feeling through which I distinguish the world and my place in it.

I preferred to regard the resemblance between my sibling and myself as the work of creation in a hurried and uninspired moment. Perhaps the resemblance was passing in the way there may have been similarities at one time between myself and others in my family tree. Meanwhile, my sibling and I greeted each other a couple of feet apart.

※

I worked so long on my first poem that it settled in the storehouse of my memory. Lodging there, the text won the authority to represent my inner being, due to its fortitude if nothing else. My feeling of self-worth was reliant on these few lines of text. At this time in my life, I was doing a fair amount of harm to myself and would go to the city at night, and at very late, or early, hours, I would end up reciting this poem to someone. Once I recited it to a person in a dangerous occupation, and, in return, I was given a kiss. I confess that the kiss gladdened me in a way that I have not felt since. Though my listener may have taken my age into consideration and offered more encouragement than I deserved, perhaps my inexperience leant my poem an authority I continue to possess.

＊

I was in my own bed again. My mind was following into sleep some fragments of speech that lacked placement. It was remnant language that needed situating for my rest. Through that cloud arrived a few words, a token of solace to redeem for a few hours' sleep. (My solace does not need to be complicated, especially for my own soul ever since it began burning through my body toward articulation.) Though the speech of my imminent sleep required no breath, I of course did when pulling myself back into consciousness, reaching for anything to write with, and writing those few words, requiring no more than a few letters, on the nearest surface. Whatever judgment I had in semi-consciousness determined that these words had broader placement.

I then fell back asleep for eight hours. I spent that time within unclassifiable depth, and while waking, was lifted to an existent haven that was identical to my surroundings. My face was veiled by daylight. I felt, on quite a cellular level, an isolating luminance around my face and haircut. It felt to bolster the tenderness, not entirely removed from violence, wherein I would be brave enough to approach you. It was bright enough around me for there to be no question of my blushing in that solitary moment.

＊

My mother would wait at the train station for my arrival from the city. I did a lot of living in the moment between spotting her and seconds later being spotted. This caesura was the most difficult part of discovering how much we had aged. I wanted immediate recognition but was never about to call across the room: the bustle made by passengers seeking familiar faces would have overwhelmed my voice. I instead approached silently to deliver myself from a city's filth into my oldest union. I approached from a community of solitaries dispersed.

❇

I was kissed on the lips by someone who knew the ways of enacting joy in countless others. It was a soft and wet kiss that created within me a sensation of floating. I wanted to float and continued to do so. While heading home, I pursed my lips toward my nostrils to smell what was left of the kisser's scent. Hadn't my lips always been shaped by desire in unexpected fashions?

With my lips in this position, I had the sensation of having disappeared up my navel. The wind carried smells that interfered with my intended scent, but I gave my surroundings no attention. I would sooner spit out my lungs. It was a city where I was prepared to applaud a kiss that could invade it like nature. It was nature where I was prepared to applaud a kiss that could invade it like a city. I was not due any time soon to fail and fade from what was demonstrated on my very mouth.

❇

I lie down, and my heart gently knocks whatever I rest on my chest, and I adjust its balance with a light touch. (It is unknowable whether I am lightly guided so that I balance better.) Objects I balance must accommodate the well-meaning contours of my chest and the circulatory system that my contours enclose. What appears to be my immobile body is, if not a destructive thing, then something with that potential. Here I wish to indicate that whatever force is found in its modest, even metaphysical, dimensions carries the potential for much more harmful acts. It is only in repose. The space it occupies displaces so much, not just the possibility of my absence.

❋

I am finite between two kinds of infinities: whatever is larger and whatever is smaller than me. One can, after all, keep looking for things larger and larger, or things smaller and smaller, in an inquiry that never ends. What else am I but a station of a particular size, a site of countless appearances and disappearances by friends and thoughts, strangers and procedures? Though I am certain I am finite, there are perhaps an infinity of finite things that shape me. There is the finite size of my body when sitting still, or of my thought on a certain topic, or of my voice when joining a tune. These sizes vary, but the type of inquiries I prefer can go on unknowingly.

❋

Everything I wear undergoes an observable transformation once thrown onto me—a human clothes hanger—for jaunts through cities, deserts, forests, and seas. The substances my almost obliging materials absorb include everything under the sun, and moon, not to mention those exuded by my body, by the nine most notable and troublesome holes on me, or the small infinity of minor openings along me, making of me, and the rest of us, the space through which our exertions pass.

Because things encounter my body and things are expelled from it, doesn't that mean that everything collides on my body's surface and openings? If so, my clothing is witness to many of these encounters, because I, a human clothes hanger, am always in a state of accepting and expending: such is the entirety of what I have accomplished to this day.

Considering the gaps between our atoms, and the vigor of my
encounters, it surprises me that the bodies I meet and draw against
me or myself into do not pass entirely through me. I manage to
return home in one piece through what I can only call kindness.

＊

I sometimes lock eyes with someone on the street and feel something
inexplicable begin coursing through me. Where this inexplicable
something originated is an inquiry I have not had time to pursue.
Instead, I dissect the phenomenon and use the adjective *arrow-
struck* to describe myself in that moment. If I had to use that word
in a sentence, I would say: To lock eyes with another on a busy street
in the sunlight can reduce all the world's trajectories to that glance
and leave someone *arrow-struck*. Radiating through one's brilliant
corporeality is the material of and response to that arrow, along with
whatever the arrow was dipped in before striking.

Any sensation is a gift. In this moment, I was given the gift of
transforming into a piece of struck flesh humming from the sight of a
bearing so tranquil that I would not dare interrupt the receptivities
of our rather beautiful, even animal, constitutions.

＊

Study of one's physical limitations does not always entail making
very good choices. Lessons arrive when one is harmed, throws their
body into risk or pain, eliciting the exhilaration of feeling one's
limits, then greeting them with one's skin or deeper. The body is
resilient, and we should discover that fact. It is better to do this
when younger and defenseless, before injuries accumulate and
cannot be outgrown.

I have a few that have resided a while with me. Through them, I
perfect caution, which will be a great help when my body breaks

down further, when my reflexes atrophy, when my bones thin, when I truly am threatened.

We must maintain at most an atom or two of our essential dignity. It is important we lose much of our dignity, but we still need those one or two crucial atoms, or three, to feed ourselves and maintain respect for the living while keeping aware of the dead, who circulate through our genes looking for ways to help and hinder the firing of our neurons. (It obviously requires several generations for a body to be rid of an ancestor. Some say it requires seven.)

When making an existence for ourselves, the positions and phrases we use bring about a correction according to the world, the cruelness and goodness of others, in spare time or on the clock. It becomes difficult to fathom that these are the same tissues, muscles, and organs from conception; they have only been translated.

✳

Then there was the decade I spent reading a thousand books. My brain was delighted by being swaddled and entombed by the alphabet. The brain-text encounter evoked structures and impressions like I was a passenger contentedly fallen into distraction. I maintained a steady reading pace, almost athletic, whether I was stretched in bed or walking a street, so that I, with hope, could uninterruptedly complete a reading session lasting ten pages. I compulsively stopped my session on a page number that ended in either one or six; otherwise, my quantifying impulse, which oversaw my chase to one thousand books within the decade, began to bother me.

At times, the pleasure was too great to slow my pace. Other times, I was only looking for language to steal, which I did. Or I was dying to escape the moment outside my book's confines. I never left the library, whether it was at home or in my backpack while I traveled.

When reading, I used the light touch of a pencil to mark passages that would represent the sum of my so-called study. It was as though I were designing a defense for myself. Whatever shape my defense was to assume would exist in those marks, because I read distractedly and forgot instantaneously like a conduit or automated thing. There could very well have been at the entrance of my memory an eraser that wiped clean the text of the pages. Due to this eraser, I could never be called on to speak for my reading, and I wondered what would happen if I tried to write everything I remembered and every impression I experienced regarding a book I just a moment earlier had finished. I doubt the text would be very long.

If I was asked about my reading, I required a few moments to answer, and, while my face slackened to betray a kind of idiocy, I struggled to recall the most recent book's cover, weight, design, and, yes, even the contents. To recall the name of a book's protagonist was a special triumph. With the pencil's notations, I set outside myself my memory, and that, with hope, will offer me the answers to any inquiries, especially when the books I have written appear uncertain in handling the matters continually set before me.

☀

I was in the front row before a singer whose voice resounded through my body. I saw the bottom of the singer's shoes, the stitching in their attire, and the contortions of the mouth overseeing and handling the hardships of delivery. Then I realized I had chosen a seat that was ruinously close. Once I saw the potential for an atom of the singer's saliva hitting me at a crescendo, presumably on accident, I reddened with embarrassment. It was obviously a proximity I would refuse to abandon if given the opportunity, though I wished at times I were forced farther back.

My enthusiasm for the singing worsened my predicament. What registered as a singer's small gestures of acknowledgment made me want to act out and possess the singer entirely yet imperceptibly. I placed my hand over my heart to indicate where the singer should direct their voice. The piece that had registered so well, even transcendently, on my dimensions started to fail. My behavior annulled our consummation, and I became immobilized by humiliation, a kind of intimacy almost no one desires.

I wished I were a listener invisible to the singer but just as near. Perhaps then I would have radiated a purified desire.

✳

When seeing my favorite singer in concert, I became a column of listening. The walls receded, giving way to the divisions set by my singer's phrasing, which delayed or accelerated each lyric. The singing redrew the grounds where my future converted into present experience, and I was aware of the displacement. I was alerted to time passing. My present was that of the singer, who altered each song's phrasing so that I could no longer whisper along. My lungs were either rushing ahead or falling behind the revised phrasing.

The voice I failed to align with reverberated through my torso. My soul looked upon the scenery of this system. It was really why I decided to attend. The phrasing of my body, always going about things with its own rhythm, consistent with my species, found an adjustment in my singer's rearrangement of my present and my location in it.

✳

Without my body, my soul is going nowhere, just as without my soul, my body is staying put.

I straighten my back, put on my jacket, and find my means of praising diminished.

The day causes diminishment within me.

World, where are you, someone might be saying, but of course any sound I hear tells of a world.

The range of my hearing is far, and sometimes I find myself so amazed at something spoken that my mouth gapes.

I may look instantly emptied.

My stillness can only be called a refinement or ideal.

*

I am probably, by now, the age of my mother and father when they were awaiting my birth. I am sensing the development of something at turns indecorous and genteel. I may have the unspeakable wish to cut the vital cord, see my family line die out, or stunt my family tree, perhaps because I am not impressed by some who preceded me, or I cannot honor their work or nurture anything into my present dimensions or qualities.

I may only bring about a different inheritance, bearing a few traits of the lineages I have known, though they may not biologically be mine.

*

I began my autobiography to get it out of the way. I expected to live many more years, but enough memories and sentiments accumulated that I felt the desire to contemplate my behavior and the miracle of my presence, which is the common miracle of anybody's, and I thought a text could achieve this. I also thought, *It is best to get this out of the way now in case something happens later to make me incapable of getting it out of the way then.* I began to twist conclusions about life into garlands of expression, which I pinned to the ceiling of my room. In the moments I committed my pencil to whatever paper I could find, I held my breath. Though I may not have known what words I needed, perhaps I should have looked at *and, could, mine, not,* and *the* then proceeded from there. I wanted to narrate the entirety of my life so that even whatever happened to me after its completion was somehow addressed. All else would be spoken for by design. I said to myself, *Perhaps I will have written myself out of a body.*

❋

All I have attempted is a cyclical practice. To cohere through all my changes, what I shed and discharge, develop and grow, I do not require my passing materiality, or my excretions, or my current appearance, none of that; rather, I would like to return to my starts inflected by the work and what has been done to me.

Though my life will not repeat, I make a life from *beginning again* in circumstances populated by my previous presences, shown one another, greeting or ghosting, vital beneath my skin. Such introductions make of my past presences a collective. It acts, and I go on examined.

❋

At the party, I praised the cake only to be told that it came from the worst supermarket around. They sent me home with it, so I threw it in my bag and pedaled into the dead of night, a faintly glimmering world.

Like I was a passenger, my bicycle brought me past the police station where the entire world's criminals were locked up. I went past the firehouse where the entire world's burning began.

It occurred to me that some indestructible thing might be within myself. (I could phrase that as a question, but then the reader would inflect the sentence, and I do not want to make singers of my readers just yet.) The idea that I carry this indestructible thing and not seek it, I thought, is worth examining.

I would prefer to discover the relation between my blood flow and another body's curves. My pulse quickened to accommodate the incline that I pedaled, much like it would quicken when I found the one with whom to share this cake.

Approximating paradise while remaining cautious would put my feet in opposite directions.

I thought about antiquity, how people feared to cross their world's boundaries, which to others today, or yesterday or last year, appear like a stone's throw away, at most a coastline a few degrees past the horizon. I suppose I am stuck on absurd and big questions, because otherwise I would be living irredeemably.

I was taken past the laundromat spinning the entire world's washing, the hospital nursing the entire world's newborns, the restaurant setting the entire world's tables. The state of my cake was somewhere between mishandled and crushed, working its way, irreversibly, to the second condition and likely toward more thorough mistreatment before I could offer it to anyone. My sensitivity to the tenses I used and use became and becomes yet another casualty of my distraction.

*

My days last equally long, and each is the same distance from me.

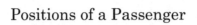

Positions of a Passenger

I see a beam of light divide a street.

I watch the traffic from a doorway and joke that the city will be shaken by judgment from the face of the earth, yet I, for one, am taken nowhere.

No one is really an only child; we are still accountable for each other according to our affinities.

It is afternoon, and noon alerts the next hour that it is leaving and gathers its things.

It gathers every bright-eyed hope of what could be shaping up, and my eye reflects loss within the world's open form.

My cashier knows what is shaping up when I need to request my penny in change.

Today it requires many more hours to earn a month's rent.

I ignore the florist because I cannot name any of those flowers.

I feel like nature and nothing like a florist.

By now I have a pocket of time, so I write in my notebook to reach a happier judgment.

I sit down and think that I am not doing my best to resist the city.

I wonder if the cashier is teaching me a lesson.

I figure I should just go it alone, leave behind the penny, and when I need to pick up someone, do it on my own.

From there, I access my capacities for adulation.

I think that nature may as well take up residence in the streets of the city.

I could never ask how much I must lose to enter an essential life of uninterrupted lyric.

Rush hour arrives, and what matters to me vanishes.

I try to tune out the police sirens.

I joke that the state sentenced to death my king then went to work on everyone else.

There are actions in this world that make me hope that judgment will come to everyone no matter how much I am doomed by that standard.

It is often a forgetful earth that the sun revolves around.

Astronauts and pilots are terrible imitators of ascension.

After this stanza, no matter that I write in prose, an hour could alert its next that my physique is not yet primed for proceeding, and that this lyric will not work well for my defense, and that there was never a plan to force my expression to resemble that of someone polite.

Consolation needs only a fraction of the time needed for one hour to alert its next.

It needs much less time now than a decade ago, and even less time now than a year ago, making me almost too young in my expenses.

It is not guidance if it cannot revolve presently.

❊

I designed my immaculate white wardrobe to say no to the world's dirt and to articulate my affection for that very same world. The nature of my encounters is legible through the condition of my clothing afterward. Any encounter carries the possibility that I will be marked by it quite visibly. A speck of anything, if fallen on an item within my wardrobe, could misrepresent me or represent me too well.

It is clear from my wardrobe that I need to make some very important decisions. When I am set on my ideal desire, extending from my ideal behavior, conversing with my sensitivities and expressing them with the joy I have been known to inhabit, clarity arises, and I am certain that I must risk the integrity of my garments to approach it and win its attention. The hunch telling me that I have found my ideal engagement creates an incredible heat throughout my body, and I break a sweat.

✳

Often I dress like those I want to seduce or be seduced by. If there is not someone special, there is always a type that models a society I wish to join, so I conceal my distinctive qualities to force the necessary similarities. Then I am allowed to enter various circles. (Flies traverse flypaper.) I mimic and converse, asking the world of whomever I attract, opening my lips to let it all out, perhaps alluding gently to our state of incompletion.

Countering this is someone whose clothing stands in stark opposition to mine. Rather, I stand in a clothing of the group I wish to defect. The figure that catches my eye cannot be won over in the way I am dressed, and I do not have enough time to run home and change. My desire makes a wound through which I lose the enthusiasm of my sartorial decisions.

✳

I thought about a certain body I had not fully known and of holding it against mine to become indifferent to embarrassment, or the absurdity of anyone's anatomy, when ingesting its scent to make the operator of that body accomplice, exchanging saliva, not to be made a metaphor or stand in for the entire populace, and instead to be seen by some and find a hollow in being seen, a profound adventure, because I would like to be sick with that body and its operator. In other words, I would like us to exist as a singular breathing.

※

However I encounter another, I might feel it hard to leave. This is the basis of our solidarity, as deep a solidarity as two organisms can reach without passing entirely through one another.

A chest or back is a barrier. By pressing against it, I communicate to it about those with whom I have shared time. Don't I find affinity when, for example, a nose like a bird can nest in a body's hollow? The one encountered might resonate through my actions for days or years.

※

The rooms where these encounters took place did not necessarily open onto our graves.

※

I sat for a portrait drawn by my love. When told to pose naturally, I found that my artist intended to uncover a hidden resemblance. Limbs distended, head pinched at the temples, eyes pushed into the skull, the drawing showed a preference for bodies that function less than perfectly. I was not sure what had been seen in me.

Once finished, we undressed in the bed that had been unmade by my modeling. (I prefer beds to be unmade by love.) In this moment, the bed was further unmade by a lick of violence that I was unable to withhold.

In a work, if no body is present, it could be said that spirit is suggested; when a body happens to be present, there is the occasion for an alternate anatomy to be brought into the open. In that bed, I was concerned with inner depths as well, but I never dared ask my artist whether this portrait looked a thing like me.

＊

I rather visit the graves of writers than the homes they occupied. (Should a writer be living, I may postpone my visit.) Each moment when I visit a writer's grave is ceremonial. I enter the cemetery with little idea of the plot's location. Walking aimlessly, I read and forget hundreds of names. I am only matching the shapes of letters that occupy my mind.

Sifting through the dead like this, as though I search an inventory or seek a face in a crowd, only increases my admiration for the dead writer whose accomplishments, if not their actual grave, exceeds those in the vicinity. I recall the writer's works while relying on intuition to navigate the slabs. I begin to tremble.

After a while, the anticipation tires me, and I may ask directions from, say, a gardener. It is heartening to report that the writer's name is almost always recognized by these types. The writer, through internment, has attained a degree of notoriety among people who may not know the writer's works.

My pace quickens as I approach the grave, and when my eyes read the name of my idolized writer, after reading hundreds of names, even my own here and there, my heart leaps and becomes solemn before the grave, its shape, material, condition, and biographical information, even an epitaph, which never honors the writer's writing, especially whenever it is extracted from the writer's own corpus.

I jealously occupy the area around the grave and scowl at arriving admirers. They are not my fellows; they are my competitors, in a sense. I kneel at the grave and touch its surface. I also understand that I am directly above the corpse of the writer I admire.

Sensations arise. They are inexplicable, perhaps a little perverse. I can only say that bodily proximity to the dead writer informs my appreciation, even my *understanding*, of the writer, in the way that it is quickest for me to access a writer's writing by hearing the writer read it aloud.

After a few minutes, the exhilaration of encounter diminishes. I wear out the welcome I gave myself, but before leaving, I must acquire a souvenir from the site. I use a pencil and sheet of paper usually reserved for my own writing to create a rubbing that lifts the writer's name from the tomb. Or I take a leaf that had fallen onto the plot. I have occasionally stolen an offering that another admirer left on the tomb, such as a flower, pen, tiny stone, or coin.

✺

I quit all but one of the arts I have practiced. I quit a few because I rarely wanted to practice. These arts never pulled me away from my life or brought me closer. Obviously, I was not staking much on this art, whereas I am always getting out of bed in the morning and avoiding my or anyone else's bed at night to work on the one art I have yet to quit, no matter my exhaustion or the consequences I face when I favor my one art over, for instance, my health. I am often deferring the necessities of living for my one art.

Another reason why I quit a few arts is that my talent leveled off. I neither improved nor worsened but occupied a plateau where I performed the same motions each time I practiced; these were motions one learns during the first lessons in the art. When one begins well with an art, others are quick to predict a bright future where one devotes an entire life to the art, but what they praise as potential is in reality plateau or peak.

I quit the art at these instances of plateau or peak because I was not able to develop any intuition to guide me. There was no inquiry. I practiced the art less and less until my early talent dissipated, though some of its motions will never be lost to me.

If I were the last person on Earth, and who knows, someday I might be, I would still be here, on Earth, practicing my one remaining art. I would practice my art to center myself within the prospect of receptivity. I continue my one last art.

✻

I train all the time for what you see me do.

After a light meal, I leave the house and imagine that my feet are pushing the ground from under me.

The sensation of rising replicates the ascent I make to vistas where I think that the air has been improved exclusively for me.

Often, I sense that the outside has undergone a great improvement and not me.

The exercises upon which my success depends look mundane, as though they are the everyday activity of just about anyone, perhaps because these exercises are the everyday activity of just about anyone.

Yet my exercises do not replicate the positions I later use; instead, I am being primed for awareness.

Areas of my body will recall these exercises, or studies, and act without a conscious thought from me.

When you see me succeed at what I do, I must look like a marvel, *a sensation for the books.*

Each area of my body articulates.

It is a phenomenon for which I cannot take credit.

Its origin is as imperceptible as the recognition I might receive, but my faith in it has continually saved me from peril and brought me a few steps from the doorway to the place where my solace has been promised—proximity can be sufficient affirmation.

*

I wonder what a life of continual inspiration would resemble. Eating and sleeping would not feel so necessary. Inhaling and speaking could happen simultaneously. In my inspiration, brushing my teeth makes me feel resentful. I am living with uninterrupted focus, my gladdest labor, then something in my hygiene requires attention. A coating, a dusting, a film has developed upon or within me.

In inspiration, I delay the essential annoyances of my upkeep, then perform them as a break from my study, a tedious caesura, a bit of rest though I resent the necessity of rest. I begin to do several things at once. I brush my teeth while bathing and think through issues of aesthetics. I read a book while walking to a restaurant so that I can feed myself. I marvel at the agility of my feet and hands completing several tasks while I think up the next moves in my project, but amazement at my body is also a distraction unless I define myself as a totality of operations within a life so that watchfulness centers itself in my heart—the sensation of something alight.

I would rather eat and sleep without the distraction of eating or sleeping. I would rather cut my hair, do my laundry, renew my passport without any effort. I rather continue along a passage of subtractions toward the stillness of contemplation. Right now, its object may be absent as I might be extinct. I go on to floss my teeth, drawing a diluted taste of blood.

✳

It is only partly true that I am seen at my happiest when I am uninterruptedly reading, because if I were reading uninterruptedly, I would probably not be in sight of anyone. I would be in total seclusion. Proximity to others while I read is unwelcome, so I might turn my back, especially to a friend, perhaps less to a stranger since no one knows what strangers can do. In other words, I make a vicious claim to space. People are eager to sit and chat beside a reader because they can talk without disturbance.

Perhaps this has been true since the very first appearance in public of someone reading on their own, defenseless against all the sounds seemingly conspiring to distract them.

✳

For the past few years, a tiny speck of matter has been floating inside my left eye. As quickly as I can, I shift my gaze several times, throwing my eyes and their contents in any direction, nearing improvisation with as much velocity as I can commit. The displacement undergone by the speck in my left eye is minimal.

✳

I have heard in concert one of my favorite singers, now quite advanced in years, almost a hundred times. It is not so much about the singer's legacy or talent, or what remains of either, as it is about witnessing someone persist in a craft despite increasing frailty and the deterioration of quality that leads an audience to lower their expectations.

Early in my concert attending, my enthusiasm had no limit, the amplified voice resonated through my body, and I committed to make it to the very end of either my favorite singer's performing career or my own career as a performance attendee—in other words, the end of my life—whichever occurred first, no matter how many years were necessary. I thought to myself, *Either I am going to drop dead or my singer is.*

Such a commitment is only made in spry times before doom closes in for a singer and concertgoers, some nostalgic, some more informed, who hold their tickets printed with the singer's name and the exorbitant, almost perverse, cost of admission. Yet it was only after the complications of the singer's old age became foregrounded during the concerts that I reached acceptance and defined for myself an affirmation to bring into my own efforts to remain a creator among the living.

In these concerts, I observed someone who happened to be my favorite singer start collaborating with the very limitations that had become a detriment. No longer was the past acknowledged. It was the sort of restrictions that other singers shy away from yet were nightly being set by my singer front and center, in emphasis. Nevertheless, out of someone's mercy, the lighting became dim enough for most ticketholders to miss the adversity that was asserting itself with increasing confidence, so I began purchasing tickets for a seat as close as possible.

✻

With others I share a made-up language. It is like a private dialect of what society speaks. Over time, it creates abbreviations, jokes, ticks, drawls, inflections, and other habits. It may reach the point where we are not comprehendible to overhearers. A made-up language, already a degradation, is at risk of deteriorating whenever my interlocutor and I part. (This is one reason why I may never want to leave someone.) When we see each other again, our made-up language must be restored. If we feel affectionate, my speaker and I lean into each other and rejuvenate this language, or if something is off, we may speak comprehendible to all, losing our intimacy.

✳

I stopped my bicycle at an intersection that had suddenly become the site of a pedestrian's death. I was catching little glimpses between bystanders and police when a fellow bicyclist said that it would be best not to look because, as it was put, I would not want that in my mind. The cyclist had already seen the body and, having that body in mind, took the initiative to impart advice, yet I remained on the side of life attempting to look through a limit.

✳

My friend and I share a phrase for a variety of conditions we see in people whose views harmonize with ours. When we refer to such people, we say that *they have the darkness*. By the *darkness*, we mean sensitivity to the trouble our species creates and an aspiration to transcend the conditions in the world that permit this trouble.

Darkness, of course, is not limited to the world but is also reflected within our very selves. Observation of darkness in ourselves is the darkness. Having the darkness implies that we are alive, and acknowledging this is to have the darkness. The best outcome is a moment here and there of transcendence, such as an affirmation of goodness or an expression of care that opens a view upon a brilliant totality that includes us.

When we see those who do not have the darkness, it is difficult to believe that we belong to the same species. It is as though they are

47

hiding something. We look deeper, ask a follow-up question, and we discover that they hide nothing. It so happens that they do not have the darkness. One is led to believe that because the world is dark, people with the darkness would be found everywhere, but I have not found this to be true. The world is dark, yes, but sometimes it is its own unfeeling witness.

※

Someone may believe that they live in dark days only to realize that, in an instant, others made it darker.

The sun rises a few hours later like an unnumbered beginning.

One may wish to stand up to the situation.

Yesterday's exercises to strengthen the legs and arms have new uses.

Others look at people and notice aspects that deserve opposition.

Appearance overwhelms the senses while any look ventures a risk.

The ground is pulled from under the sighted.

(The ground is never larger than the dimensions of a pair of shoes.)

Some can no longer conceal their disdain; others take the day to plant trees.

Children fly kites as a means of escape.

Among them, a presence that is simply stunning has provided them a loan, as long as they are living and waiting to be called by disobedience.

The market stays consonant.

A gesture from a different life is attempted with kind motions, or by feigning to wander through a world before its time.

Today, keeping still is necessary to watch the motion of others, their works and transformations.

＊

When the darkness is most evident, I try to adopt one of the following views. Each is a misapplication of the darkness. One view is that despair is part of the human condition, if I may introduce here the fact that I am human. To feel this way means that I am alive. That I am overcome with this sensation implies perseverance, but to turn and face despair can diminish the energy I need to find an affirmation. I am raw within it, immobile.

Another point of view is that my despair is only the product of neurons firing, in my case misfiring, because my immediate wellbeing is not under threat. Such are the workings of my brain. I might decline a doctor's prescription on the assertion that the despair of this moment is my natural state, and to alter it would be unfaithful to my very being, but I am saying such things then cutting my hair or nails, or wearing a black jacket to stay warm and show the world that I have the darkness.

Another point of view is that I should nevertheless express gratitude. My heart breaks, I fall within the fissure, so I should turn to that that gave me the opportunity to collapse. There is the hope that I will be restored, if not to the undivided goodness of the world then at least to my prior ability to stand, better yet, to move within it and make friends. The darkness indicates a void, and in the moment it is closest, I am to direct my strengthlessness toward turning the void into a fulcrum where through I elevate myself.

I was born with or given very early the intuition that the potential for reconciliation is always present. I have had a few instants with it. Sometimes I wonder if reconciliation arrives toward the end of one's life, at the very end, or after, and it is a matter of remaining positioned so that a darkness can be extracted. I am discovering lessons of attentiveness.

✳

I feel as though different alarms are going off within me. With all this noise, a body like mine starts to tremble inwardly. It withdraws but wishes to enact goodwill outwardly.

After all these years, my wish to resist continues to knock within me, as though it requests entrance somewhere.

The alarms within me continue what they were built to accomplish. I feel reluctant to create, though I always claimed that it would determine my solace. In the past, I felt that I had an eternity to get it right; it was as though installed inside me was a language machine capable of outliving me.

✳

I might benefit from an invention that I could hold to my mouth and speak into so that, through an instantaneous process, whatever I speak would be comprehendible to anyone, no matter the languages they know. To be effective, this invention would remember talkers' habits, corresponding their phrases across languages while cataloging the entirety of its users' input across time, demonstrating that language is a living thing, mutable yet traceable, almost self-correcting, giving one the impression that language contemplates itself.

This system would not suffer interruption by any user's death, even less my own, considering the disservice I have committed upon language. An invention like this is a step beyond the systems and archives and customs that contain the imprint of our voices and thoughts, correcting the mistakes that bring about uncomfortable situations. I would also love an invention that could express what I have been unable to articulate, making me comprehendible to any listener, especially those I wish to bring closer.

✳

It can be improper to smile in public; no one knows the latest news. When a story reaches me, I may have been absently smiling, then the corners of my mouth slacken with exhaustion from and affection for all of you. To see cheerfulness in public after the news might make me feel raw. I cannot even have a guest over because the entire public is in my home. I shape a beneficent likeness of what I want to witness. It is possible to do this from a single, ordinary chair.

✳

That we breathe and hear involuntarily, this suggests that we are still persuadable.

✳

After getting knocked off my bicycle, I felt more shame than bruising or swelling. I felt embarrassed of my poor reflexes and brakes, and the stream of words I spoke.

Everything was an insult to what I call my physical integrity. Taking a moment to determine my injuries made me feel like a sad and helpless animal. I, immobilized, dressed in black as though I anticipated the occasion, felt fear amidst an agile public.

Most of all, I could not deny that the accident indicated that I have failed in what I call *my life of attention*. My behavior, more human than I hoped, showed strangers that I was ill prepared for this life. I had lost sight of the object of my pursuit.

＊

My romance has ended and will not return, so I sort through our made-up language. Though the language is not extinct, the number of practitioners has diminished by half, a calculation I reach through the understanding that this missed one is not coming back; whether the one who is gone thinks of our conversations, or of me, is not an important inquiry. I convince myself that I no longer exist in the mind of the one who is gone while the one who is gone has installed themselves in my thought.

Our made-up language is then something I speak on my own within a culture of one. It is sustained by the affection I still hold for my gone interlocutor, who, in my thinking, responds to my complaints and questions in a way I find characteristic of the original person. I stay conversant despite the danger of lapsing into recitation, the fate of all dead languages.

＊

Sometimes I show up in public like anyone, though I am subject to a different weather system called solitude. My skin slickens with my exertions. My form loses its uniqueness to a fog. I cannot count all my bones and impulses, but it must be a tremendous number that is always changing. I would not know where to begin.

In these places, I might realize that, no, I am not alone. In that system outside me is another pedestrian who has decided against keeping some distance between us. The sound of this one's stepping mingles with that of my own. Our four feet syncopate then devolve into clatter. It occurs to me that this pedestrian's two feet are attempting to fall in step with mine. How else would we botch it so embarrassingly? If I could slip into a steady rhythm, I would be in one by now.

To bring one's self to a stillness that another can approach is not a gift to be just handed off; it is the sensation of amounting to, or working toward, a totality, or a shared destiny. These are things everyone knows; I am just not explaining them very well. Whatever ensues with a stranger, provided that this other pair of feet is attached to a stranger, a transposition is completed, and the air becomes visibly altered.

❋

At times, I am someone arriving home at dawn from what might simply be a one-night stand. I immediately begin a note to counter that potential. Though exhaustion may cloud my thinking, the expression of my affections for the one I just left cannot be deferred. My eloquence is sometimes flawless on occasions that call on my so-called heart—it is up to the recipient to recognize this eloquence. I make no careless marks in my composition. I finish my note and hope it will have its desired effect.

Then a beam of daylight brings attention to the condition of my clothing: a distraction that counters my eloquence. My clothing reached a sorry condition in the mess and motions of winning over another. I look fondly at what I wear then move to send the note against every wave of fatigue.

❋

Shot through me is the writing of someone I never knew who died in an epidemic. Somehow when I am reading, as though it were the author's hope, my body is weakened and soon thrilled. That the author lived elsewhere in another decade is no matter to my penetrability, my belief that we both could have made it.

The writing's preemptive love with its reader is evident, as are its offer and intentions. I should have been born in that other time to get my nose out of this book and into a hollow along the author's body, a bid to deepen our intimacy, risking its corruption and exasperation, though I have been willfully seduced, in premeditation, perhaps to bring my author some comfort while lying in bed during those dark moments that no one should face on their own.

✳

It was said that it is possible for someone to become so defiled by the world that they would be unrecognizable to family. I offer myself as example.

If I return now to my family, I would look quite changed, transformed not only by time but also injuries from the world, its work and inertia. If they would accept me in this state, they would potentially accept anyone pulling off a decent imitation. Somebody could step forward with enough understanding of me, maybe one or two facts, not much of a routine, and probably take my place.

There are a few reasons an imposter might succeed. First, although my substitute does not need to mirror me trait for trait, our injuries would look similar: the world injures person A and person Z with similar methods. Second, our injuries would match whatever worried families expect; we spend our lives contradicting their irrational fears because we wish to enjoy the irrational worlds that try to destroy us, and they sometimes do destroy us. Third, when spoken to, I always looked at my shoes.

✳

The question of what one has become during the time away cannot be answered. It is good to suspect that the transformation goes deeper than the filth of one's clothing or bad posture.

Perhaps while away, one adopted the better qualities of one's hometown. In a way, it is absolute goodness that brings us into being, bends our ear to whomever speaks a similar merciful phrase or just a phoneme of a phrase that is on the verge of crossing entirely into coherence, or collapsing, half believed, onto the hazy border between that very same coherence and its opposite, though adjacent, country.

✳

I am composed of distances I try to diminish. One could put a hand on my chest to feel those distances within me exerting pressure.

From my perspective while moving, the world has not gotten worse, but it has not gotten better. I try to approach everyone with a courageous humility. Some are bold enough to remain among the likes of me, and I wonder who they are. Others increase their distance from me, and I wonder why that is.

I wonder if, whenever someone saw me in my infancy, they realized I would, as an adult, become a recipient of their animosity or of their care. The distance I am from my infancy increases at the rate that I approach my future reconciliation. I am being pulled forward from a specific point in the future that I cannot yet anticipate from here.

✳

I may not hear it, yet I expect an approaching train whenever I see anybody running to the platform, so I begin to run as well. Punctuality is as much a concern of spirit as it is of logistics. If the train pulls in when the two of us reach the platform, I picture being commended at my destination for arriving on time. If the train's arrival is wrongly intuited, error bonds the bounder and me, and our waiting on the platform embarrasses us to the point of intimacy. Our tardiness has yet to be reconciled, and the sight of us panting together makes that clear to everyone.

✳

Forgetting where I am for a moment, I am only a passenger within human anatomy, rather, human-enough anatomy. If I register sensation, I become it, or its resonance, slurring my surroundings if I am speaking, or blurring them if I am watching.

Then I regain my bearings and confirm that I am indeed a passenger, though to be specific, I am a passenger on a train that is moving. I change into that passenger, a visible adjustment, and my surroundings appear for me to meet them. I might even enjoy the company of these fellow travelers, but probably not. Our arrival requires no effort of our own. It creates the present stillness wherefrom we leave.

✳

A tourist should wear their old clothes and discard them along the way.

Luggage will lighten as the fatigue of travel deepens.

In the street, sunglasses should be worn regardless of the weather.

After several days in one place, locals will ask for directions in a language that still sounds foreign.

A tourist will have lost all bearings.

It is quicker to get directions from people selling things that no traveler would be expected to buy.

No matter one's confidence, ordeals such as public transit and restaurants will become a pageant of ineptitude.

Gloating over earlier success will vanish.

A tourist should never carry along their passport.

Carrying a notebook to immediately record impressions can prolong the present.

It is like never leaving the photo booth discovered underground.

Whether someone's staring originates from hatred or desire is hard to determine, but there are tried-and-true approaches to reach clarification.

Then a tourist may wake up someplace else.

Also good to keep in mind is the distance between points on the itinerary and their altitude.

Never talk to the police.

Speaking can rarely redeem one's self to others, though a local might ask why a tourist is still in town.

When that question is asked, recite a few compliments about the place, its people, sports teams, food, and architecture.

The following day entrusts itself to our care.

It arrives in our hands and rests clean for the moment.

Shoes fall apart, but a tourist should resist purchasing footwear: new shoes get broken in at the expense of the feet wearing them.

These and similar pains are a reflection of our second self that everyone will see and shy away from.

Having been a companion all along, this reflection is introduced to us when we travel, perhaps by way of our displacement.

My admonitions are not traps; even if they are, making them resonate is the task of our households.

✳

In a foreign country, I started a romance. I was visiting from a wildly permissive town. My new friend was also from abroad but from a nonpermissive place. I could go as far as saying that in the city where we met, the prospect of oppression had been suspended. Here my friend was subject to less violence. I had intuited this through local newspapers. What was not clear, however, was the degree of permissiveness that I had lost. I said to myself that it was not a significant loss since I had enough degrees to spare. My passport allowed my return. My money was the same color as theirs.

But we were still required to be watchful. Some types, perhaps, would be nuisances from time to time. Accompanying a body that was often in danger gave me the feeling that I had been under guard throughout my life. During our sightseeing, the only word I recognized was the one for light, because I am (just barely) monolingual. Inside churches, little branches from local trees were available for a donation.

At night, I became quite acquainted with this one's torso and that hollow forming a juncture between spine and skull. My nose fit well within that hollow. This one when undressed was discovering a security that I always enjoyed. The hotel room was a satellite of a haven that I occupied daily. If this is homesickness, I thought, I must marry everyone in danger overseas.

I saw in this romance someone whose chronology was much shorter, not only because I was older, and from a permissive town, but also because danger had germinated in my friend a quickly burning yet defiant radiance. My romance's self-preservation extended to mine. The pain of my almost excessive freedom was being revealed.

＊

I sometimes get the feeling of watching the world, or whatever happens to be outside, go by. If it is the world outside, so be it.

It is as though a great favor has been done for me. When bicycling, I am beside myself with little need to touch the pedals. My mouth is too distant, so another is speaking in my place. Another is crashing on my bicycle. My wounds are suspended inches above the surface of my body. Though it looks like my hand, I cannot even tell whose it is that takes yours this very moment.

When not existing, I am existed upon. Or I am made a passenger. Crediting me for my arrival accounts for only one side of the union through which the life I love, mine, is sustained. This union's other side situates a body that compliments my own: a stranger I approach, for instance, or an incarnation I may or may not recognize.

＊

When I buy souvenirs, a small inversion is made in the world. I anticipate my room filling with items from places that its windows will never look upon. In souvenir shops, the absences on the shelves carry my initials, though my payment is no correction to the lineage of pillagers who preceded me.

Pillagers and I have similar interests. We hope to stay on schedule. We try to make each step a tribute to a past we barely grasp. We also worry that we will be charged more than the locals, somehow impacting the authenticity of our experience.

Whereas pillagers brought back incredible artifacts, I am known to settle for cheap baubles from the most tasteless shops. Almost anything has the potential to preserve my recollections. At the very least I will have the memory of shopping.

Too often I worry that the inside of my skull and whatever it looks upon when travelling will lose all trace of the sensations I want to keep. I worry that I will lose the sensations that make travel my preferred way to live.

✳

I write my biography and lose interest in who I am. I am not performing an autopsy or life study. I might be past examination.

Not to disappear up my navel, I am staying responsive to the world from the quiet of my room.

All I should be concerned with is direct address, speaking on behalf of the age I reach. I am only sentimental when I delay sharpening my pencil.

✳

My subject must be whatever is now peripheral to my vision. It should never be lost upon my sight's alignment.

✳

Creation was more than I could accept.

Elation was more than my habitat.

✳

Like a wilderness that has no keeper, I walk among countless living things—grains, herbs, roots, and trees; mollusks, insects, eggs, and critters—and realize that we are captive, domesticated to no owner, and thrown upon each other to replenish the world through fucking or erode it through exertion.

It is hoped that the sun collects with its beams everything they reveal, along with all else that is hidden, and retain us in perpetual observance directed particularly nowhere.

Here I am returning to a common refrain, though isn't repetition the nature of pleading?

❋

On Earth I stayed. And distances within me exerted pressure.

❋

When despair about the world grows in me, on me grows an ecology.

Any part of my body is precedent. My eyes exemplify the rippling seen in shallow pools inhabited by the smallest lives, even singular cells, and where roaming animals refresh themselves. All are welcome to rest around my eyes and whatever has taken root.

At each of my collarbones is a chasm with shade. Beneath are the blood vessels and nerves that assist my structure. Unheard-of colors are seen on the flora and fauna found on and inside me, a terrain of musculature and fatty deposits.

The rolling of my hips is a place of relaxation; the pits of my arms two sources for watering. (I always spill essential materials when making my love comprehensible.) Blooms extend from damper regions, so beehives later appear, little economies in air. My eardrums may rupture from their buzzing, but I have been busy, too, marking my methods of self-preservation; this includes replenishing my fluids so that you can find me fecund.

The hollow of my groin attracts forms known for their resilience through the seasons. A few are familiar, though often, they are not.

My legs, covered like others with a light down, have hardened from everyday activities in curtailing my terror. These legs are negotiated by climbers and traversers intent on lengthy journeys. There they may learn obedience around the places I am tattooed, a scarring synonymous with testimony.

Any living thing can approach me, but I would never let them grovel at my feet, because it is often my feet that resist my conscience.

You must take me as just one erotic and neurological, sensate and creative totality: one nose, two eyes, two arms, two legs, ten fingers, ten toes, though my description here becomes presumptuous: I have not recently verified these figures.

When despair about the world grows in me, on me grows an ecology.

✳

People believed that Earth was the center of the universe because they were not thrown from it, nor had they seen anyone else thrown from it. I suggest I have been thrown from Earth because none of us should be the center of anything other than a reference to the outside. This intuition is the gravitational pull into the core of my society, the care of those who negate the harm of others. Sensations arise by perfect design. When I approach others, my ambulating is little more than a series of tremors in my knees, ankles, and feet.

✳

At the eclipse, the temperature dropped, animals knelt, and people cheered while darkness set over the morning. I identified closer with the animals, though I also had humans in mind, particularly the anonymous masses from antiquity, not too far passed, those unlikely beings who shook throughout the phenomenon and read in it terrifying prospects.

People around me cheered because they understood the science behind the eclipse, though I remembered that others in antiquity understood the science so well that they predicted eclipses within what we today call an hour or two. I was suspended among several timelines, including that of humans today, the most likely of beings, who ooh-and-ahhed away the eclipse, though their predecessors took appropriate measures to appease the force or forces they were witnessing, and they secured themselves. These predecessors may not have been too mistaken, though I do not wish that I was born in their time.

At totality, the darkness that fell upon us appeared not like a sunset but a sun's extinguishing, a mini-extinction that would result in ours. The moon carried an aura of fire, and like the otherworldly, offered no insight into people's chances of survival. In the darkness, I started taking steps from the crowd with almost alien movements, loosening myself from affiliation.

Your Life

If I could suggest a form of life, I would point to the image of a fly adhered a few inches above the drains in urinals. The facsimile is responsible for preventing human spillage. Visitors who presume a living fly direct their stream upon it according to a supposed hierarchy of living things. Much to the visitor's wonder, the steadfast fly dismantles that hierarchy, and this quality would need to be emphasized in my suggestion.

Resembling a corpse, you quieted flies; they wanted nothing to do with you. A form of life was developed against the present buzzing among us.

Yet the targets of my piss (and worse) are numerous. You suggested a method that would leave me still standing and speaking, reshaping my mouth to announce my extinction, not only to antagonism but to many of my actions and thoughts. Let me find your gestures turned into my reflexes.

✳

The contents of our two skulls could cover acres, refuting a subtractive atlas with a fertility that reversed the extinctions around us. You said we would be recognized as allies because we traversed these places with a care that preceded us. It was tenderness we fulfilled.

Flawed thinking could hurt us, lay its teeth into our smooth necks, but we were cautious, even behind closed doors when grooming ourselves, lying in bed, or introducing each other's breath into one another's circulatory systems, a sort of translation.

When the desire between two bodies is set in motion, society, imprinted by encounter, experiences an adjustment.

✳

I could have said that the world outside our door was bleak, though I did not want to question your decision to settle in it.

By the word *world*, we should only have meant the smallest circle inscribed upon a globe, with our room as its center and extremities. Outside it, you and I would have been of little consequence, really just a perfect duo of nobodies.

✸

What will be the form of our lives so that I applaud you until my hands bruise? Entering the masses who welcome you, even when they do not realize that they welcome you, I would feel no violence despite the crush against my chest. I would hold my breath until I found an opening for air, or a representation of innocence.

What will be the form of our lives so that I make sense of this at the instant my joy is tendered, no matter whether my heart splits? Though all this implies I am injured, instead may I be recomposing, explaining how you understand what I and my fellow passers-by cannot, though we are vibrant nonetheless, in our practice and joy, through forgetting or fondness, and throwing ourselves into it.

✸

You bring me such joy that I could shake a tree to make whatever is in it sing. In a populace of correspondences, we stand poised to do so. If you are in the right mood, we never need prompting. Such is your influence. If you think of water, I could turn into a fish. I hear all of nature making requests, and I write them down. When reading them over, at what point do I realize the present sentence is a question requiring an upward inflection?

✸

When you are away, the world approaches. It falls at my feet, out of its senses, inarticulate, a reality. I see its potential, everything that could be accomplished if I join it again. The world holds my attention. There are moments when I join it, and healing begins immediately upon the injury. Other times, however, I wish that you'd return, since your arrival would chase out my unwelcome occupant, this native invader. I wonder how it entered, whether I somehow asked it over. My page becomes dirty with speculation, a step I will incorporate into the process if this happens again, and it probably will, since I am not yet ready to leave home. (My body is like a transmission waiting to be sent.) To acknowledge an intruder then return to what I was doing might be the clearest expression of my fondness.

*

When you and I were together, you lay in my arms, and I wished to occupy the position for a little longer.

When you checked for my pulse, I found a form of life.

Up to the day we met, the world's conditions were preparing of me a body that could spend this life together.

When you bandaged my bleeding, I understood I was already prepared by my intuition.

You put your hand to my chest, occupied my openings, dragged me from the pit, dressed me to meet your mother.

The strain of my muscles was a matter of articulating these situations, the weakening of my resistance.

*

We spent enough time together to amount to a life. You still appear to me a wonder. I refer to what you said to inform my discipline and disobedience. We faced losses that couldn't impact the likes of us. I gambled and lost your money, poured and spilled your drink, picked and spoiled your blooms. I owe you all these back, though I continue to lack the essentials we declined, such as sleep and breathing.

If it was violence that loitered outside, we toured our rooms. I buzzed my hair close and threw the clippings from the balcony, then we put on black clothes. Styled for self-preservation, we walked out into society. Shame in our lives was unhelpful. If there was an outside world then, we still meant to float within our conversation. It was love and less importantly a model for living.

Each part of your body articulated. I made a habit of observing you when you were eating, drinking, pissing, fucking, walking, standing, sitting, sleeping, waking, speaking, and keeping silent. I could feel myself being seen doing the same. A watchful moment was a unit of measure, as was the length of our limbs, or our tongues.

We rested against one another; it was a sign of our resilience. I relied on you in my independent study, and you carried my work in your pocket. It wasn't amazing that the sum of my labor could fit in a pocket but that you chose *my* work to carry with you. It made no difference whether our thinking was universal or only verifiable on the ground that our shod feet occupied. I replicate it by asking the same questions we posed to each other, and expecting your responses, I sometimes reach that fugitive feeling.

✳

Like everyone, I am arriving and departing at once. My home steps out of the house when I do. It stays within me. Through these motions, I discover where it is that I sweat, and if I may confess, there is not one inch on me that has held back when I turn toward you. All my exertion must make me appear like a blooming, or a little explosion, within my human totality—if the look on your face, a composite of all faces dear to me, gives any indication.

Aren't I expending myself out of a body until I am all absence? When arriving and departing at once, the days last equally long. Sunday approaches a Monday with promise that Tuesday broadens for Wednesday's realizations for Thursday to sway to a restful Friday for the reflections that occupy a Saturday wherein I am stilled and all days are the same distance from me. I am not existing; I am being existed.

✳

You make for the two of us a passing world, so there is no time to compose a eulogy for every cell of ours that expires.

When you indicate a form of life, my biography becomes no longer expressible to me.

I choose you to resume my narration, and if you don't begin in the following moment, I will not assume that my life is over.

I trust that you will start later, maybe when a clearing centers itself in our flux, a quiet moment to begin again.

In this request, I won't yet be pleading, so I speak like you are in the room, or I speak to you silently, or I write to ask that you resolve my trouble.

When I listen—no matter that I look inattentive, incapable of learning, at one with idiots—a word from you is enough to orient myself, to break my being, to make a coffin for the worse facets of myself, such as my helplessness.

Forget the eyes and whatever it is you show me (it passes): the ears are respondent organs of affection, by far.

It is unimportant whether I lose these sights and words; their feeling will still be had.

✳

In the encounter between you and I, there must be, mustn't there, an image of goodness within at least one of us, or it must be outside us and available for invoking. It remains to be seen whether we can triangulate with that goodness and avoid calamity. (This must be as difficult as countering gravity.) Wherever it is located, that goodness, I figure, could triangulate with us so that each side is congruent and its effects almost totalizing. Our faces would begin to appear alike.

✳

Before I found you, I felt my possessions to have been finalized: a desk, papers, and enough books to comprise the slimmest library, the barest conversation between texts. I carried that library, one volume short of a curriculum, through every hour's breaking news. *Only a city where one can lose one's self is worth its name*, I thought.

What I carried was effectively the sum of my learning, the attainment of hours spent in my small room. Prepared with this sum, I found you in the midst of extinction, and we began to negotiate.

✳

I am most content when I appear as your mysterious arrangement of the pile of atoms creating my physical dimensions.

✳

I wonder if I make appeals to you because you resemble me. If you no longer resemble me, at one time you did, and might once again, and

72

it is in that time I have you: my ideal of union. My injuries and victories correspond to yours—if they happen to be my best.

Your attraction is found in your forms and greetings, the wishes you have for the world. I reach out to touch your face. My behavior is carnal, disembodied, a romance in a landscape upon an anonymous continent. Your dimensions reopen the question of your attraction: the erotic, ethical, extraworldly faces that you show at the juncture of two moments.

✳

I only hope that when I speak, I appear to you like a column of meat and breathing, exalting and decomposing, having woken to necessity. I speak, though no one else, as far as I can tell, can fulfill that necessity. I could empty my lungs here and now. All I hope for is finding before us the interplay of our most tender receptivities.

✳

My written line transposes my body's willed and unwilled motions; the content of that line transposes my thought. I do not want my handwriting to be admired, only its potential to articulate your brilliance.

✳

Perhaps I am only composed of syllables you have spoken. I write *perhaps* because you have not said so. Instead, I have heard your apologizing, correcting, crying, debating, enthusing, eulogizing, exclaiming, flirting, insulting, praising, protesting, stuttering, warning, etc., and sometimes I have seen your very own body while these occur, the violence and tenderness you give and receive, never a balanced equation because you are so generous.

Sometimes I think that, besides me, there is no one else who has stopped and thought about you in this way, and at those stopped and thinking moments, I hear within me those syllables you spoke.

Maybe I am an archive who has set the limits to the circulation of these syllables. I say *limits* because I haven't chosen to go *everywhere*.

If each syllable has its say, my own voice becomes the minority, and if I happen to speak an entire phrase of yours, I only embody your intentions for that moment.

※

You could still intervene with a word, impact my society, reshape it to my, or our, ideal. It must exist within my reach because it cannot exist elsewhere.

I may not know it, but you rely on me to create that word's potential. It would not get far without the prospect that it will occur to me. It wavers on the tip of my tongue or ricochets in my ear. I could hear it from someone I speak to because there is no other way for them to reply. I might turn from my route and be met with it.

When I come into this kind of contact, I press myself into its articulation, no matter whether my form can accommodate its contours. Then I proceed like a living commemoration. I hear such a word, and my head brightens. You see, you and I cannot afford to be in dispersion.

※

I see you in various forms. Often I recognize you so that I have found a companion. If I only see a few of your qualities, I may suspect that I have found you, then I approach along grounds that I wish were more certain.

I might be wrong. These faults cannot be ascribed to either you or me. That must be a thing you might tell me; we'll see. When I cannot see a trace of you, I bow under the weight of your absence, as any friend would.

Our opportunities and deficiencies are the same but only occasionally converge. Though you are in sight, I am still asking, *What is this?* You stay on the threshold of resemblance. Perhaps you should just say it is you, or at least agree it could be—that would save some time.

＊

Could however I describe you equal its negation? I must do so to prove the life you variously manifest. When that life was shown to me, I hoped to broaden the associations my language creates, no matter whether this language is understood by others.

When I say that your arms are around me and that they are not, I speak to the limits we face whenever we are together. The limits of my language are far worse. If I am ever to speak properly about you, these connotations must change.

I require passage by my negations into a benevolent articulation. I intend to praise you. When I say that at once you arrest and release me, I speak to the flux of our life together.

My definitions are determined through usage. Before me, you will be found my articulation. And I will be putting my mouth to yours.

＊

Why do you separate me from the earth?

I had just sat down to lunch when you pulled me away to resume a conversation I thought we finished.

I wasn't ready to admit that my intuition has yet to turn into reflex.

It remains in that middle zone of uncertainty.

I wear my jacket of nothingness and turn up its collar against the cold.

My chest is a dark engine that operates on things I only seize with cruelty.

I was out with friends when my hearing was taken over by another scrap of your narrative.

The turns in your stories straighten my spine.

When you begin one, I anticipate a sudden ending, and my life is lengthened.

It is not necessary for us to greet each other in the world, but when we do, I see you pulling me out of it.

You slip an arm around my waist when I am walking to a date with someone who leaves me indifferent since you persuade me so well.

You prepare me for the terror I may someday meet; if it is not terror, then it is elation.

I might be taken out of myself so that the light you tend to is no longer obstructed.

❋

Each morning, you answer the question of your life by shuffling the branches of your lineage.

I would not be the first to break a small twig off a bough and, waving it before everyone, say that here is the entire tree.

✳

Maybe you change into other living things, or act on their behalf, or it is simply a joy to say so. It is as though you substitute yourself for different parts of creation by stepping across the limits between us, and them, then gift me the intuition to say so.

Unable to trace your shape, I prefer you surround me, your presence overflow my sight, humbling me and the qualifications to my correspondences, while I remain displaced and unresolved, isolated in my dimensions, wondering if I could join what I observe—

You steady my attention so I see that you put me in motion. I watch you hold on to what is unquestionably within you.

✳

I ask my senses to only select whatever traces your movement. Only your fingerprints should be found on my instruments. Artifacts of your speaking should nestle in my ears. All these inform my thinking: a rupture and rapture, a sense of escape. I shift my definitions and ascribe again each usage. I remove from my mouth whatever it surrounds and break my teeth on your reasoning.

In this way, I should see neither for myself nor for others. I should reach nothing that meets the requirements for selfhood. I should turn to you and leave my shelter; I should not stay in a place that I cannot own.

You prepare me for the day I extract from myself whatever you refuse to inhabit.

✳

To have your narrative might be just enough for my exaltation, however often I may fail to alter my actions, turn a phrase to your timbre, or escape things, and though thinking that the narrative is true is not necessary to find one quite noticeably changed, receiving fresh exposure to an undivided life, I sometimes wish to think it true and have even felt that the whole narrative is not so far-fetched since it is the chronological rendering of resensitizing, which I need many days of the year, if not every last day of the year, however many days that turns out to be, though I will need to continually approach that narrative and find it beginning again within me through each hour and more exceptional moments.

＊

When I first laid eyes on you, I knew we would spend a life together, but not mine, at least as it was or continues to be.

I can only articulate the possibility of this life, so I do not know why I tried to account for my past and present.

My promise to you is as yet unarticulated.

I allude to the incomplete form of a life, that I committed an error in this writing, or so I would confess if it were not for how I clarified my desire.

＊

When you pulled me out from it, I brought with me the shock and stink of revival. Everyone else either covered their mouths or their children's eyes—I hadn't thought so many could be present. The account of my return would be an offence. My mouth would recall how my arrival got to stink of perspiration and traversing: a brio. Humus and pus were at its center. Also at its center was the friendship between the two of us. It was ratified by your weeping. When you pulled me out from it, you bent my chronology into circularity, the circularity of return. Any opportunity for autopsy was over.

✳

You asked me what was on my mind, and I said that I was thinking of how to reply. When you asked, *To what?*, I said, *To how you indicate a life.* I also said, *It's difficult to follow the tenderness of your ethics.* You said, *It's not about imitation but sustaining the care shown by your friends.* I asked, *Even shown by me?*, and you stepped back and said, *No, not quite you. Maybe a moment from time to time.* I kicked the ground and asked if this moment occurred because you were present, a reminder, and you answered, *I would not have been able to watch you otherwise.* I agreed. There was a pause in our conversation, though all else continued. By this time, it was dusk, or it was dawn, and a passage opened within me, and I said,

✳

ROOF BOOKS

the best in language since 1976

Recent & Selected Titles

• THE COURSE by Ted Greenwald & Charles Bernstein, 250 p. $20
• PLAIN SIGHT by Steven Seidenberg, 216 p. $19.95
• IN A JANUARY WOULD by Lonely Christopher, 90 p. $17.95
• POST CLASSIC by erica kaufman, 96 p. $16.95
• JACK AND JILL IN TROY by Bob Perelman, 96 p. $16.95
• THE RESIGNATION by Lonely Christopher, 104 p. $16.95
• MOSTLY CLEARING by Michael Gottlieb, 112 p. $17.95
• THE RIOT GRRRL THING by Sara Larsen, 112 p. $16.95
• THOUGHT BALLOON by Kit Robinson, 104p. $16.95
• UN\ \MARTYRED: [SELF-]VANISHING PRESENCES
IN VIETNAMESE POETRY by Nhã Thuyên, 174 p. $17.95
• POLITICAL SUBJECT by Caleb Beckwith. 112 p. $17.95
• ECHOLOCATION by Evelyn Reilly, 144 p. $17.95
• THE RECIPROCAL TRANSLATION PROJECT
by Sun Dong & James Sherry. 208 p $22.95
• DETROIT DETROIT by Anna Vitale. 108 p. $16.95
• GOODNIGHT, MARIE, MAY GOD HAVE MERCY
ON YOUR SOUL by Marie Buck. 108 p. $16.95

Roof Books are published by
Segue Foundation
300 Bowery • New York, NY 10012
For a complete list, please visit **roofbooks.com**

Roof Books are distributed by
SMALL PRESS DISTRIBUTION
1341 Seventh Street • Berkeley, CA. 94710-1403.
spdbooks.org